Tiger Talk
Get Into Science

Water Play

Leon Read

W

FRANKLIN WATTS
LONDON • SYDNEY

Contents

Look out for Tiger on the pages of this book. Sometimes he is hiding.

Water is a liquid.

Water feels wet and slippery.

Safety Notice: Children should never be left unsupervised when playing near or in water.

Water fun

Water is fun to play
with on a sunny day.

What happens when Maria is squirted with water?

Water containers

Which container holds the most water?

The spotty one.

The stripey one.

Andre uses a measuring jug
to find out who is right.

Using water

Water is very useful for...

drinking,

...washing,

moving.

10

What other ways do we use water?

Water from the sky

Water that falls from the sky is called rain.

Sam is making
his own rain.

Where does the
rain water go?

Staying dry

Sometimes we do not
want to get wet.

Waterproof materials keep us dry.

wood

clay

metal

glass

plastic

What waterproof materials can you think of?

?

Floating and sinking

Some things float,
and some things sink.

Andre puts some objects into a bowl of water.

	sink	float
plastic brick		✓
pencil		✓
marble	✓	
wooden brick		✓
coin	✓	

Sinking feeling

Rabbit's boat is on top of the water. It is floating.

Tiger adds some marbles.

The boat goes under the water. It sinks.

Why did Rabbit's boat sink?

Solid ice

Very cold
water changes.

I'm going to put
my lollies into the
freezer.

The water freezes.

It becomes a
solid called ice.

What happens if you don't
eat your lolly quickly?

21

Water colour

Make a bubbly water colour picture like this.

Mix paint, water and washing-up liquid in a bowl.

Blow the mixture with a straw.

Place a sheet of paper over the bowl. Lift it up — see what picture you have made.

Word picture bank

Drinking – P. 10

Floating – P. 10

Ice lolly – P. 21

Rain – P. 12

Squirt – P. 5

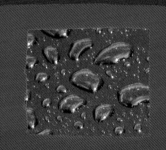

Waterproof – P. 15

First published in 2007 by Franklin Watts
338 Euston Road, London NW1 3BH

Franklin Watts Australia
Level 17/207 Kent Street, Sydney NSW 2000

Copyright © Franklin Watts 2007

Series editor: Adrian Cole
Photographer: Andy Crawford (unless otherwise credited)
Design: Sphere Design Associates
Art director: Jonathan Hair
Consultants: Prue Goodwin and Karina Law

A CIP catalogue record for this book is available
from the British Library.

ISBN: 978 0 7496 7618 6

Dewey Classification: 553.7

Acknowledgements:
The Publisher would like to thank Norrie Carr model agency.
'Tiger' and 'Rabbit' puppets used with kind permission from
Ravensden PLC (www.ravensden.co.uk).
Tiger Talk logo drawn by Kevin Hopgood.

John Eder/Taxi/Getty Images (4). Klaus Hackenberg/zefa/Corbis
(15l). Kent Meiris/Image Works/Topfoto (3). Pixland/Corbis (10tr).

Every attempt has been made to clear copyright.
Should there be any inadvertent omission please
apply to the publisher for rectification.

Printed in China

Franklin Watts is a division
of Hachette Children's Books,
an Hachette Livre
UK Company.

There are 17 Tigers, including me, in this book.
Did you find all of us?

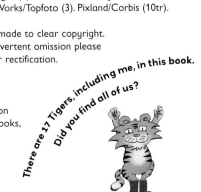